ideals

AUTUMN

In joy I watch the woodland leaves
Adrift in jeweled jamborees.

Parading banners twist and fly
Into the shimmering, sun-splashed sky;

Rich colors whirl from treetops bare,
Their beauty burning hazy air.

In autumn breeze they tumble down—
Vermillion, gold, and chestnut brown.

Elisabeth Weaver Winstead

Publisher, Patricia Pingry
Editor, Peggy Schaefer
Art Director, Patrick McRae
Production Manager, Jan Johnson
Editorial Assistant, Kathleen Gilbert
Copy Editor, Joan Anderson

Front and back covers by Gene Ahrens
Inside front cover by Fred Dole
Inside back cover from FPG International

ISBN 0-8249-1064-8

IDEALS-Vol. 45, No. 6 September MCMLXXXVIII IDEALS (ISSN 0019-137X) is published eight times a year,
February, March, May, June, August, September, November, December
by IDEALS PUBLISHING CORPORATION, Nelson Place at Elm Hill Pike, Nashville, Tenn. 37214
Second class postage paid at Nashville, Tennessee, and additional mailing offices.
Copyright ©MCMLXXXVIII by IDEALS PUBLISHING CORPORATION.
POSTMASTER: Send address changes to Ideals, Post Office Box 148000, Nashville, Tenn. 37214-8000
All rights reserved. Title IDEALS registered U.S. Patent Office.

SINGLE ISSUE—$3.95
ONE-YEAR SUBSCRIPTION—eight consecutive issues as published—$17.95
TWO-YEAR SUBSCRIPTION—sixteen consecutive issues as published—$31.95
Outside U.S.A., add $6.00 per subscription year for postage and handling.

The cover and entire contents of IDEALS are fully protected by copyright and must
not be reproduced in any manner whatsoever. Printed and bound in U.S.A.

Thoughts on Autumn

Nathaniel Hawthorne

Still later in the season Nature's tenderness waxes stronger. It is impossible not to be fond of our mother now; for she is so fond of us! At other periods she does not make this impression on me, or only at rare intervals; but in these genial days of autumn, when she has perfected her harvests and accomplished every needful thing that was given her to do, then she overflows with a blessed superfluity of love. She has leisure to caress her children now. It is good to be alive at such times. Thank Heaven for breath—yes, for mere breath—when it is made up of a heavenly breeze like this! It comes with a real kiss upon our cheeks; it would linger fondly around us if it might; but since it must be gone, it embraces us with its whole kindly heart and passes onward to embrace likewise the next thing that it meets. A blessing is flung abroad and scattered far and wide over the earth, to be gathered up by all who choose. I recline upon the still unwithered grass and whisper to myself, "O perfect day! O beautiful world! O beneficent God!" And it is the promise of a blessed eternity; for our Creator would never have made such lovely days and have given us the deep hearts to enjoy them, above and beyond all thought, unless we were meant to be immortal. This sunshine is the golden pledge thereof. It beams through the gates of paradise and shows us glimpses far inward.

Photo Opposite
AUTUMN IN VERMONT
Int'l. Stock Photo

Birches

Robert Frost

When I see birches bend to left and right
Across the lines of straighter darker trees,
I like to think some boy's been swinging them.
But swinging doesn't bend them down to stay.
Ice storms do that. Often you must have seen
   them
Loaded with ice on a sunny winter morning
After a rain. They click upon themselves
As the breeze rises, and turn many-colored
As the stir cracks and crazes their enamel.
Soon the sun's warmth makes them shed crystal
   shells
Shattering and avalanching on the snowcrust—
Such heaps of broken glass to sweep away
You'd think the inner dome of heaven had fallen.
They are dragged to the withered bracken by the
   load,

And they seem not to break; though once they
   are bowed
So low for long, they never right themselves:
You may see their trunks arching in the woods
Years afterwards, trailing their leaves on the
   ground
Like girls on hands and knees that throw their
   hair
Before them over their heads to dry in the sun.
But I was going to say when Truth broke in
With all her matter-of-fact about the ice storm
(Now am I free to be poetical?)
I should prefer to have some boy bend them
As he went out and in to fetch the cows—
Some boy too far from town to learn baseball,
Whose only play was what he found himself,
Summer or winter, and could play alone.

BIRCH TREES
Geoffrey Clifford
Wheeler Pictures

One by one he subdued his father's trees
By riding them down over and over again
Until he took the stiffness out of them,
And not one but hung limp, not one was left
For him to conquer. He learned all there was
To learn about not launching out too soon
And so not carrying the tree away
Clear to the ground. He always kept his poise
To the top branches, climbing carefully
With the same pains you use to fill a cup
Up to the brim, and even above the brim.
Then he flung outward, feet first, with a swish,
Kicking his way down through the air to the
  ground.
So was I once myself a swinger of birches.
And so I dream of going back to be.
It's when I'm weary of considerations,

And life is too much like a pathless wood
Where your face burns and tickles with the
  cobwebs
Broken across it, and one eye is weeping
From a twig's having lashed it open,
I'd like to get away from earth a while
And then come back to it and begin over.
May no fate willfully misunderstand me
And half grant what I wish and snatch me away
Not to return. Earth's the right place for love:
I don't know where it's likely to go better.
I'd like to go by climbing a high birch tree,
And climb black branches up a snow-white trunk
Toward heaven, till the tree could bear no more,
But dipped its top and set me down again.
That would be good both going and coming back.
One could do worse than be a swinger of birches.

Carnival Time

Zenith Hess

Autumn is a carnival,
A final, joyous fling
Before a silent, white-robed sleep
Weighs spirits down 'til spring.

Red sumac by the roadside
Flies banners in the breeze,
And golden fragments swirl and drift
Beneath old poplar trees.

In the orchard, ripe fruit speckles
Every drooping bough;
And in the hedge, the bursting grapes
Hang low and tempting now.

Flower gardens blaze with blooms
Of scarlet, bronze, and gold;
And roadside stands are heaped with gourds
And pumpkins to be sold.

Vines in treetops bend and sag
With clusters overhead;
The maple tree has changed its gown
From emerald to red.

'Mid festive panorama,
New spirit fills the air;
We celebrate our harvest yield
And autumn's bounty fair.

Photo Opposite
FARMHOUSE IN VERMONT
Bob Taylor

As Imperceptibly As Grief

Emily Dickinson

As imperceptibly as grief
The summer lapsed away,
Too imperceptible, at last,
To seem like perfidy.

A quietness distilled,
As twilight long begun,
Or Nature, spending with herself
Sequestered afternoon.

The dusk drew earlier in,
The morning foreign shone,—
A courteous, yet harrowing grace,
As guest who would be gone.

And thus, without a wing,
Or service of a keel,
Our summer made her light escape
Into the beautiful.

Autumn's Glory

Kay Hoffman

When summer fields turn tan and lean,
Then autumn comes upon the scene,
Splashing hills with red and gold—
A dazzling picture to behold!

Flower beds are lavish, too,
Dressed in vivid, festive hue,
And overhead an azure sky
Is brighter than in mid-July.

Tall maple trees along the lane
Wear rainbow halos once again
As field and meadow overflow
With harvest gold God's hand bestows.

A purple haze on distant hill,
Tawny waves on a grassy field,
Sunset's flame of red and gold—
Breathtaking beauty to behold!

I bow my head in praise and prayer
'Mid autumn's glory everywhere;
No other journey is so grand
As when Autumn takes us by the hand.

Photo Opposite
ASHLEY NATIONAL FOREST
UTAH
Tom Fridmann

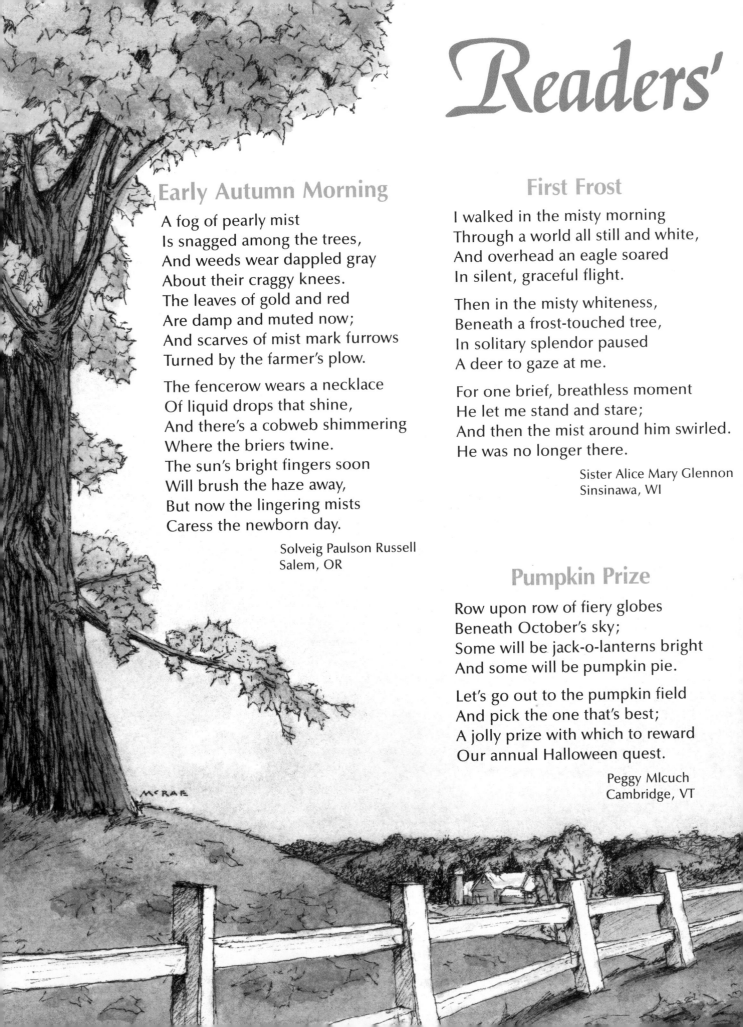

Early Autumn Morning

A fog of pearly mist
Is snagged among the trees,
And weeds wear dappled gray
About their craggy knees.
The leaves of gold and red
Are damp and muted now;
And scarves of mist mark furrows
Turned by the farmer's plow.

The fencerow wears a necklace
Of liquid drops that shine,
And there's a cobweb shimmering
Where the briers twine.
The sun's bright fingers soon
Will brush the haze away,
But now the lingering mists
Caress the newborn day.

Solveig Paulson Russell
Salem, OR

First Frost

I walked in the misty morning
Through a world all still and white,
And overhead an eagle soared
In silent, graceful flight.

Then in the misty whiteness,
Beneath a frost-touched tree,
In solitary splendor paused
A deer to gaze at me.

For one brief, breathless moment
He let me stand and stare;
And then the mist around him swirled.
He was no longer there.

Sister Alice Mary Glennon
Sinsinawa, WI

Pumpkin Prize

Row upon row of fiery globes
Beneath October's sky;
Some will be jack-o-lanterns bright
And some will be pumpkin pie.

Let's go out to the pumpkin field
And pick the one that's best;
A jolly prize with which to reward
Our annual Halloween quest.

Peggy Mlcuch
Cambridge, VT

Reflections

September Again

Keen rays of sunshine
Pierce frosty air
As splendid new colors
Are splashed here and there:
  Crimson on hilltops,
  Rust on the plain,
  Copper in valleys,
  And amber on grain.

Our hearts brim with gladness
As all Nature proclaims,
  "Behold Autumn's glory—
  September again!"

Esther F. Thom
Worthington, MN

Perspective

I feel his chubby arms around my neck;
  With a toothless grin
  He splashes a sticky kiss
  On my forehead.

He and I, alone,
  Are romping through an autumn field,
  Enjoying rich golds and crimsons,
  And each other.

I wonder why I ever longed earnestly
  For mere silver or gold
  When an infinite treasure
  Is already mine to hold?

Geraldine Nicholas
Edmonton, AB

Editor's Note: Readers are invited to submit unpublished, original poetry, short anecdotes, and humorous reflections on life for possible publication in future *Ideals* issues. Please send copies only; manuscripts will not be returned. Writers will receive $10 for each published submission. Send materials to "Readers' Reflections," Ideals Publishing Corporation, Nelson Place at Elm Hill Pike, Nashville, Tennessee 37214.

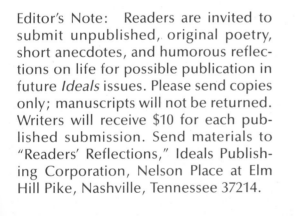

Country Chronicle

Lansing Christman

Sing softly, September . . . Sing with your whispering winds and murmuring rills, your brooks babbling over stones . . . Bring out your chorus of birds . . . Yours is a song of benediction and invitation, a fond farewell to summer, a welcome to autumn with its crisper hours.

Yours is a soothing lullaby that puts to rest a land tired and worn from a season of work . . . It eases gardens to sleep, woodlands to doze, meadows and fields to languish bare.

Let your song ring when morning dew cleans the air of haze . . . Let it free the skies of lingering clouds . . . Let it transform the heavens to rich blue again . . . Let it herald a brighter sun and glittering nights.

Weave your magic chords, delicate as the spider webs glistening on bush and weed . . . Let your wavering strains flow like the drifting leaves of woodbine and maple, the blooms of goldenrod and aster.

Sing softly, September . . . Pour out each tremulous strain.

Gently I will turn each page; quietly I will follow every note . . . Your melody is from the hymnal of the year, old as the ages, sung forever.

Photo Opposite
GRAND CANYON NATIONAL PARK
Arizona
Jeff Gnass

Scampering Leaves

Grace Autry

The falling leaves of gold and rust
Are scampering in the street;
Stripped of shade is the maple grove
Where once we loved to meet.

When Mother Nature wields her brush,
Pastels are cast aside;
Only bold, flamboyant hues
Are scattered far and wide.

But soon she'll paint the landscape white
And vivid colors hide,
Leaving only bright-clad skiers
Dotting mountainsides.

And can I never choose one best
From all four happy seasons?
As dancing leaves now fall to rest,
I know God has his reasons.

Mysterious As Promise

Alice M. Swaim

Today, I walked our winding woodland
    trails,
Scuffing gold tattered autumn leaves aside,
And watched them dip and scud like fragile
    sails
Borne on some vagrant, accidental tide.
I let the wind blow dreams like weightless
    leaves
Along the tortuous channels of my heart,
And wondered how the anchored heart
    conceives
Strange destinations not on any chart.
I held a golden feather, like a shell
Discovered on some secret stretch of sand,
Mysterious as promise and farewell,
Or sea-sound hinting of some lotus land.
Then sudden wind, like an inflooding tide,
Erased my footprints from the countryside.

Wild Life

Grace Noll Crowell

I like the quick bright movement of wild
  things:
The unexpected flash of hidden wings,
The gold torch of a squirrel's tail flaming
  high
Against an arch of blue, bough-fretted sky;
A chipmunk's scamper through the autumn
  leaves,
The brown-striped pattern that his body
  weaves
Among the blowing grass; and down the
  slope

I like the action, the stiff-legged lope
Of startled deer; and from a mossy bog
The sudden splash of a green wide-
  spraddled frog;
The dart of iridescent dragonflies;
And oh, forever, wild wind from wilder
  skies
Sharp in dark branches where the leaves
  are thinned . . .
I think of all wild things I love the wind
More than anything that is set free—
There is something in it close akin to me!

Nature's Transition

June C. Bush

Autumn's arrival has left its mark,
On each field and flower and tree,
As more of gold and less of green,
Increases daily by degree.

From verdant carpet over earth,
To first faint yellow turnings seen,
Nature works her slow transition,
As day by day, gold blots out green.

Stems and grass stand stiff and straw-like,
Thus autumn terminates the show:
Leaves that once were green above us,
Are now golden and lie below.

Belated Violet

Oliver Herford

Very dark the autumn sky,
Dark the clouds that hurried by;
Very rough the autumn breeze
Shouting rudely to the trees.

Listening, frightened, pale and cold,
Through the withered leaves and mold
Peer'd a violet all in dread—
"Where, oh, where is spring?" she said.

Sighed the trees, "Poor little thing!
She may call in vain for spring."
And the grasses whispered low,
"We must never let her know."

"What's this whispering?" roared the breeze,
"Hush! A violet!" sobbed the trees,
"Thinks it's spring—poor child, we fear
She will die if she should hear!"

Softly stole the wind away,
Tenderly he murmured, "Stay!"
To a late thrush on the wing,
"Stay with her one day and sing!"

Sang the thrush so sweet and clear
That the sun came out to hear,
And, in answer to her song,
Beamed on violet all day long.

And the last leaves here and there
Fluttered with a spring-like air,
Then the violet raised her head—
"Spring has come at last!" she said.

Happy dreams had violet
All that night—but happier yet,
When the dawn came dark with snow,
Violet never woke to know.

Photo Overleaf
TULE LAKE WILDLIFE REFUGE
California
Ray Atkeson

Birds of Passage

P. McArthur

When the maples flame with crimson
And the nights are still with frost,
Ere the summer's luring beauty
Is in autumn glory lost,
Through the marshes and the forests
An imperious summons flies,
And from all the dreaming northland
The wild birds flock and rise.

From streams no oar hath rippled
And lakes that waft no sail,
From reaches vast and lonely
That know no hunter's trail,
The clamor of their calling
And the whistling of their flight
Fill all the day with marvel,
And with mystery the night.

As ebb along the ocean
The great obedient tides,
So wave on wave they journey
Where an ancient wisdom guides;
A-through the haze of autumn
They vanish down the wind,
With the summer world before them
And the crowding storms behind,

October

Helen Hunt Jackson

Oh, suns and skies and clouds of June,
And flowers of June together,
Ye cannot rival for one hour
October's bright blue weather.

When loud the bumblebee makes haste,
Belated, thriftless, vagrant,
And goldenrod is dying fast,
And lanes with grapes are fragrant.

When gentians roll their fringes tight
To save them for the morning,
And chestnuts fall from satin burrs
Without a word of warning.

When comrades seek sweet country haunts
By twos and twos together,
And count like misers, hour by hour,
October's bright blue weather.

Oh, suns and skies and flowers of June,
Count all your boasts together,
Love loveth best of all the year
October's bright blue weather.

Partnership

Gloria Weber Henbest

They bring their child to me
And hope I'll come to know
How much the offspring means to them,
Their trust in me bestowed.

They bring their child to me
With love and hope and pride,
Looking for a helping hand,
A teacher who will guide.

They bring their child to me,
And our partnership is clear:
To nurture and allow to bloom
A life we both hold dear.

They bring their child to me,
A step toward letting go
And trusting in God's special plan
To help the child to grow.

Back to School

Kathleen Y. Bergeron

So very rare and precious,
They can't be bought or sold;
For what they give is priceless—
Worth more than any gold.

Their gift cannot be measured
Till past its youth it grows
Within a vessel never filled—
An endless quest to know.

They take the aimless fires
With which we're all surrounded,
And see that those "live wires"
All end up quite "well grounded."

Other jobs earn prizes,
But none can mean as much;
For teachers channel children
With guiding, loving touch.

Cross-Stitched Eyeglass Case

Ann Marie Braaten

Materials Needed:

8" x 10" rectangle of cream Aida cloth, 14-count
Tapestry needle #20
Masking tape
1 skein DMC floss #326 red
2 skeins DMC floss #322 blue
¼ yard blue broadcloth
¼ yard 3-ounce bonded polyester batting
Blue sewing thread
Embroidery frame or hoop (optional)

Step One: Cross-Stitching (see diagram)

Bind edges of Aida cloth with masking tape. Fold Aida cloth horizontally and vertically to find center. Secure cloth in frame or hoop, if desired.

As you cross-stitch, begin and end threads neatly from behind. Avoid using knots. Use 2 strands of floss in 18-inch lengths. Keep the direction of stitches the same (see illustration), so that crossover thread is consistent.

Thread tapestry needle with red floss. Start cross-stitching at the center and work rows back and forth toward each narrow end of Aida cloth.

With blue floss, start cross-stitching near the center, working rows back and forth again. Stitch toward each narrow end of Aida cloth until all the blue area is covered.

Step Two: Cutting Case Pieces

Measure from the border of the finished cross-stitched Aida cloth to ½ inch all around the design. Cut along this rectangle.

Cut the blue broadcloth to form the eyeglass case back (5 inches by 7¾ inches).

Cut the lining (9 inches by 7¾ inches).

Cut two rectangles (5 inches by 7¾ inches) from the bonded polyester batting. This will form the soft interlining.

Step Three: Sewing Case Pieces

Position and pin the following pieces together in order given: one batting piece, the broadcloth back, the cross-stitched front (right side toward broadcloth), and the remaining batting.

Using a ½-inch seam allowance, machine sew the sides and bottom. Trim corners. Press side seams open. Turn to right side.

Fold lining to form a rectangle measuring 4½ inches by 7¾ inches. Using a ½-inch seam allowance, sew side and bottom seams. Trim corners. Press side seam open.

Step Four: Finishing the Eyeglass Case

Slip case inside lining and pin right sides together. Sew top edges of lining and outside fabrics, leaving a 3-inch opening along the eyeglass case back.

Pull the eyeglass case and lining through the opening. Press lightly. Tuck lining into eyeglass case. Hand sew the opening along the eyeglass case back.

Are you creative? Do you design your own craftworks?

Readers are invited to submit original crafts ideas for possible development and publication in future *Ideals* issues. Please send query letters with idea to "Craftworks," Ideals Publishing Corporation, P.O. Box 140300, Nashville, Tennessee 37214-0300.

Upon acceptance, writers must supply design, text instructions, and sample product. Payment will vary and will be upon publication.

Photo Opposite
EYEGLASS CASE
Gerald Koser

Cross-Stitched Eyeglass Case

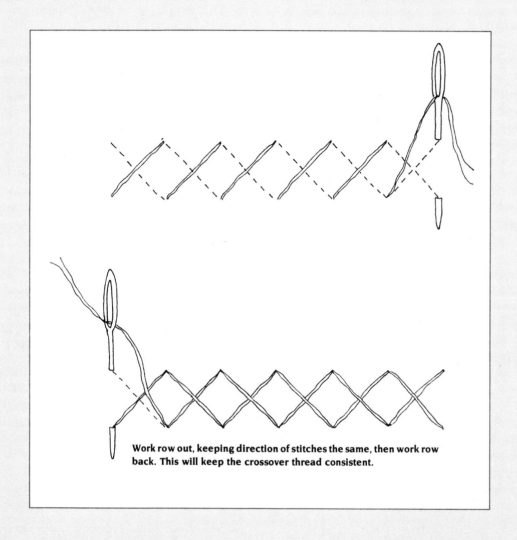

Work row out, keeping direction of stitches the same, then work row back. This will keep the crossover thread consistent.

Grid represents 14-count Aida cloth. Dots represent blue thread; X's represent red.

Old Apple House in Autumn

Grace Noll Crowell

Seeping down from the cracks in the knotted ceiling,
And lifting from the depths of the earthen floor,
An oddly released and subtle scent comes stealing
From the hoardings of many an autumn gone before.
And now afresh the Pippins, Baldwins, and Russets
Heaped high in bushel baskets add their scent
To linger long in this ancient house long after
Their color is gone and their brief earth-life is spent.

Out of an orchard whose feet are ever wading
Ankle-deep in a glittering mountain stream
Have come the apples, crimson and green and golden,
As the bright fulfillment of some man's ancient dream
Of sturdy weighted trees whose abundant fruitage
Would gleam like lighted fires across the gloom
Of autumn days—waiting the inevitable hour
To be gathered close in the dusk of this mellow room.

Old Apple House in Autumn from *APPLES OF GOLD* by Grace Noll Crowell.
Copyright 1950 by Harper & Row, Publishers, Inc.
Reprinted by permission of Harper & Row, Publishers, Inc.

Photo Opposite
JONATHAN APPLES
H. Abernathy
H. Armstrong Roberts

Sunset

Brian F. King

In the hallowed hour of sunset,
Flaming colors streak the sky,
And a drowsy birdsong lingers
Where the creeping shadows lie.

Gold and rose the still horizon,
Gentian-blue the hills afar,
Velvet-black the tranquil river
That reflects the evening star.

Oh, there's no place under heaven
Dearer to my heart's desire
Than a valley steeped in twilight
Where the sky's a band of fire.

Fall Promise

Louise Pugh Corder

Trees arrayed in gowns all bright,
Geese that honk in southern flight,
Nippy nights and brisk, fall days—
Earth with beauty is ablaze.

Farmers gather in their yields,
Corn and pumpkins from their fields.
Children play in leaves fresh-raked,
Begging fall's last apples baked.

Earth is fired with gold and red,
Though she will be put to bed.
God gives vivid promise true—
Spring will see earth born anew.

An Autumn Song

John White Chadwick

Comes the pleasant autumntime,
    And the leaves are growing brown;
Loosened from their summer,
    They are softly wavering down.

What a carpet warm and bright
    Make they in the sheltered ways!
What a splendor on the hills,
    Filling human hearts with praise!

Countless as the upper stars,
    Asters glorify the sod;
And the gentian, crisp and cool,
    Lifts its slender cup to God.

Homeward from his ripened field
    Goes the farmer's loaded wain,
Ruddy with the orchard's yield,
    Yellow with the golden grain.

Oh, the bounty flowing free!
    Oh, the beauty sweet and rare!
Let the nations do as they will
    Nature, thou art good and fair.

Autumn Blessings

Earle J. Grant

Yellow autumn is here again
With frost embossing the windowpane.
Silken corn shocks point up high,
And at their feet, gold pumpkins lie.

Wild geese fly overhead in a vee;
Flaming maples are a sight to see.
Asters burn purple upon the leas,
And ruddy apples hang in the breeze.

We lift to God our hearts in praise
For blessings in these autumn days!

October's Glories

Beverly J. Anderson

October has come with its glories,
A storehouse of treasures to share;
Unmatched is its pageantry's
    beauty—
No other month can quite compare.

Gone now are the warm days of
    summer,
Soon winter will pay us a call;
But now we delight in October—
The gold interlude in the fall.

Such splendor we'll always remember
Long after the autumn is past;
Preserved in our showcase of
    memory,
Its glories forever will last.

Hearty Autumn Casseroles

Broccoli-Cheese Casserole

2 10-ounce packages frozen broccoli, cooked, drained, and chopped
1 **cup grated Cheddar cheese**
1 small onion, chopped
1 10¾-ounce can cream of mushroom soup
3 **eggs**
1 **cup mayonnaise**

Preheat oven to 350°F. Mix broccoli, cheese, and onion in a 9 x 13-inch casserole dish. Blend soup, eggs, and mayonnaise in a blender. Pour mixture over broccoli and toss lightly to coat. Bake for 30 to 35 minutes.

Variation: Add 1 cup cooked, chopped ham or chicken to make a complete meal of this casserole.

Macaroni and Cheese

½ **pound mostaccioli *or* macaroni**
¼ **cup butter *or* margarine**
¼ **cup flour**
2¼ **cups milk**
¼ **cup minced onion**
½ **teaspoon salt**
½ **teaspoon dry mustard**
3 **cups shredded Cheddar cheese**
   Sliced pimento-stuffed olives, optional
   Tomato wedges to garnish, optional

Preheat oven to 350°F. Grease 2½-quart casserole dish. Cook mostaccioli according to package directions; drain. Put in dish. Melt butter in 2-quart saucepan over medium heat. Add flour; cook, stirring until bubbly. Add milk, onion, salt, and dry mustard. Stir until slightly thickened. Add cheese; stir until melted. Pour over mostaccioli. Bake for 20 to 25 minutes. Let stand 5 minutes before serving. Garnish with pimento-stuffed olive slices and tomato wedges, if desired.

Variation: Add 1 to 1½ cups cooked, chopped ham, chicken, or turkey to mostaccioli before topping with sauce. Reduce cheese to 2 cups.

Ham, Potato, and Onion Casserole

1½ **cups medium white sauce**
1 **cup grated Cheddar cheese**
1 **teaspoon salt**
⅛ **teaspoon pepper**
2 **cups diced, cooked potatoes**
1 **pound cooked ham, diced**
1 **large onion, thinly sliced**
1 **cup fresh bread crumbs**
¼ **cup melted butter**

Preheat oven to 350°F. Grease a 2-quart casserole dish. Put white sauce in saucepan; stir in salt, pepper, and cheese. Cook over medium heat, stirring occasionally until cheese is melted. Remove from heat; stir in ham, potatoes, and onion. Turn into casserole dish, sprinkle with crumbs and butter. Bake 40 minutes.

Cheese Lasagna

1 **6-ounce can tomato paste**
½ **cup water**
¼ **cup cooking sherry**
1 **tablespoon butter *or* margarine**
¼ **cup chopped onion**
1 **teaspoon garlic powder**
1 **teaspoon salt**
1 **teaspoon sugar**
½ **teaspoon oregano**
8 **lasagna noodles, cooked**
1 **cup cottage cheese**
¼ **pound mozzarella cheese, sliced**
¼ **cup grated Parmesan cheese**

Preheat oven to 350°F. Combine tomato paste, water, sherry, butter, onion, garlic powder, salt, sugar, and oregano in a saucepan. Stir and cook over low heat until blended. Spread a small amount of the sauce in the bottom of 9 x 13-inch casserole dish. Top with half of the noodles, tomato sauce, cottage cheese, mozzarella cheese, and Parmesan cheese. Repeat layers. Bake for 30 minutes.

Photo Opposite
CHEESE LASAGNA

Robin Redbreast

William Allingham

Goodbye, goodbye to summer!
    For summer's nearly done;
The garden smiling faintly,
    Cool breezes in the sun;
Our thrushes now are silent,
    Our swallows flown away—
But Robin's here, in coat of brown,
    With ruddy breast-knot gay.

Robin, Robin Redbreast,
    O Robin dear!
Robin singing sweetly
    In the falling of the year.

Bright yellow, red, and orange
    The leaves come down in hosts;
The trees are Indian princes,
    But soon they'll turn to ghosts;
The leathery pears and apples
    Hang russet on the bough,
It's autumn, autumn, autumn late,
    'Twill soon be winter now.

Robin, Robin Redbreast,
    O Robin dear!
And what will this poor Robin do?
    For pinching days are near.

The fireside for the cricket,
    The wheatstack for the mouse,
When trembling night winds whistle
    And moan all round the house;
The frosty ways like iron,
    The branches plumed with snow—
Alas! in winter, dead and dark,
    Where can poor Robin go?

Robin, Robin Redbreast,
    O Robin dear!
And a crumb of bread for Robin,
    His little heart to cheer.

My Harvest

Pamela Kennedy

Months ago I shooed my children out the door, scattering them like seeds upon the fertile soil of summer vacation. Freed from the restraints of school and schedules, they flew unencumbered across the grassy meadows. Babbling brooks and summer showers watered them. Steamy breezes and scorching sun helped them grow. Soon freckled faces and suntanned backs appeared, and hair and limbs lengthened under summer's urging. June, July, and August nurtured my summer crop, and now a hint of autumn in the air reminds me the time for harvesting is near.

Standing on the back porch, shading my eyes in the early September sun, I look again to the fields. Tall, golden grasses wave majestically, and in amongst the bending blades I spy my summer's yield: Sun-bleached hair whips in the wind like tassels from bursting corn, and arms wave toward the sky like full-grown wheat. Dashing, dancing in the breezes, my children call to one another. Their lean bodies are strong and firm, their little heads are packed tightly with memories of long afternoons by creek banks with squishy mud and frolicking frogs. The remembrance of still summer nights, hot and bright with stars, shines in their eyes. Trees and hills and dirt and grass have been their summer habitat, and they have flourished in abandon and innocence. Bugs and birds, toads and snakes have held class in the wood's deep shades, and airy summer lessons have crowded out the thoughts of books and blackboards.

Now harvesttime has come once more. It's time to gather in my summer children; to strip them clean of summer's stains, sweet berry juices, grass and soil; to thresh the tangles and the burrs from summer hair. They must be shucked and cleaned, rolled sweet in suds and scent, then properly bound in lace and ribbons, plaids and prints.

After that, the bundling comes and shipping off to market in noisy yellow buses. They'll sit in rows all neat and ordered, ready for autumn's lessons, eyes and ears attuned to winter's whisper.

My calling brings them running now, and I stoop to gather them in my arms. What a sheaf the summer sun has yielded, another year's full harvest that will fill my barns to bursting.

The Master Painter

Gertrude Rudberg

God took the high green mountains
And the quiet valleys too,
Then painted them with color
In shades of every hue,

There were reds, browns, and yellows,
With orange in between;
The firs and lacy hemlocks
Were touched with shadowed green.

Above He tinted cloudlets
In dainty pinkish blue
Against the silver heavens
As autumn days were due.

Yes, God who is the artist
And paints the world around
Can bring to us such beauty
With brilliance, profound.

Photo Opposite
AUTUMN WALK
Bob Taylor

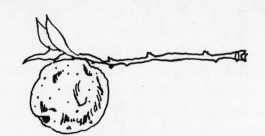

Nature's Legacy

Gene Appleby

The silence of the season settles
Gently on the land.
Deserted are the beaches where
No footprint dents the sand.

Cloudless are the azure skies;
The afternoons grow cool.
Stilled are children's voices since
They all are back in school.

Memories of summer days
Are fading fast away
As autumn makes her grand debut
In brilliant gold array.

Mother Nature gently lulls
Each garden plot to sleep,
Then blankets every patch with leaves
So seeds are buried deep.

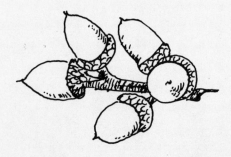
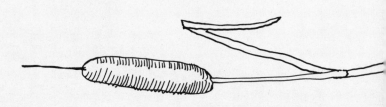

Soon shadows start to slowly grow,
Extending out of sight,
And shorn hills warmly glisten in
The darkening golden light.

Then the hunter's moon appears,
Just as soon to wane,
And Jack Frost yawns and stretches wide
Preparing for work again.

Undaunted, all creation moves
To ready for this time,
To take its place and play its part
In a greater scheme divine.

O wondrous Lord, how marvelous
Is all within your rhyme
Together in sweet harmony
Work nature, God, and time.

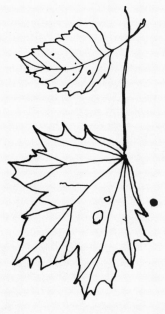

Photo Overleaf
POCONO PINES, PENNSYLVANIA
Gene Ahrens

Reflections

Fran Thompson

There is something in each of us that needs a "Walden" in order to refill the wellsprings of our lives. We need to stop and discover once again who we are and where we are going. Spiritual contemplation cannot be done in crowds, with people jostling one about. This is something which calls for solitude, for rumination of the most leisurely kind; for apartness from all things human. We must give ourselves a rest—our ears from the amplified sounds of today's "music," our eyes from the eternal conflicts on television, our hands from the busy-ness of nervous tasks.

There is no escaping the web of society of which we all are part. It is not a matter of wanting to escape it. We should want to learn how to live in it. Our world is one of tension, where conflicts are inevitable, where abrasive personalities are daily contests. The human nervous system can withstand just so much before it cries out for help. It needs to be removed from its surroundings and pampered and rested and recharged.

Anyone who has lived by the water knows the healing nature of sun and sand and sea. No one who has lived away from traffic and television and telephones will deny the soothing balm of long walks through woods, where meadowlarks and starlings and purple martins and orioles are one's only companions. Too soon, these may be only memories. A world without woods and birds and wild animals would be a world bereft of values.

I would not choose to live in it.

COLLECTOR'S CORNER

U.S. quarter, 1892

Gold coin of Roman Empire, 54-68 A.D.

Photos courtesy of American Numismatic Association

What do you envision when you hear the words "coin collector"? A bespectacled scholar hunched over a tray of glittering gold pieces? A young boy filling his "penny board" with cents from his newspaper route earnings? A businessman or woman sorting through old dimes or nickels? You're right on all counts; each of these people is a coin collector, or numismatist—a student of the science of money.

Dating back to the dawn of civilization, coins have taught the collector much about history, art, and literature. As long-lasting records of historic people and events, they offer the collector a direct contact with the past. What could be more exciting than owning a coin once held by Judas Iscariot, Napoleon, or George Washington?

Equally intriguing is the thrill of the quest and the satisfaction of finding the perfect coin to complete a collection. Some collectors search bags of coins from banks, while others hunt at coin shows or in the "junk boxes" of local coin shops. In fact, most collectors are not primarily interested in making a profit from their collections, although coins can be a good investment. The hunt and the resulting coins bring their own pleasure.

There are as many kinds of coin collections as there are collectors. Some collectors focus on the coins of ancient Greece and Rome, which often bear the images of legendary personalities such as Julius Caesar, Nero, and Cleopatra. Those with a taste for adventure (or a case of wanderlust) may assemble coins from around the world, which can be purchased at local shops. The most popular coins in this country, however, are those produced by our own U.S. Mint, which has operated for almost 200 years in Philadelphia and now has facilities in four major cities.

U.S. bullion coins

Commemorative coins celebrating bicentennial of U.S. Constitution

Because U.S. coins are so varied, many collectors specialize in a particular denomination or type of coin. For example, a beginner might strive to assemble a complete set of the Indian Head coins produced from 1859 to 1909, with one specimen from each year and mint. A more advanced collector might seek varieties of identical coins which show differences only an expert could detect. Still others might search for numismatic errors—coins which show off-center strikes or cracks, or which appear to have "bites" taken out.

Until recently, collectors have shown little interest in contemporary coins, whose designs have changed little in the past fifty years. A commemorative set issued in 1986 for the centennial of the Statue of Liberty, however, has revived interest in U.S. coinage. And an important set honoring the bicentennial of the Constitution in 1987 was the only official keepsake of that event. Gold and silver bullion coins released in 1986 in order to compete with foreign bullion producers have also proven popular.

Numismatics also includes tokens, medals, and paper money. Although tokens and medals are not sought as widely as legal tender, they are far less expensive than some popular coins.

Collecting coins can be relatively inexpensive, but requires some background knowledge to ensure a wise purchase. A numismatic novice should begin by reading a standard reference, such as R.S. Yeoman's *A Guide Book of United States Coins,* and should always carefully inspect a coin before buying it.

Collectors can also join the American Numismatic Association (A.N.A.), the world's largest coin collector's club. Members receive a monthly journal and may borrow from the association's library. The A.N.A. also offers a certification service.

Whether collecting for pleasure or investment, numismatists enjoy a unique link to the past.

Barbara Gregory

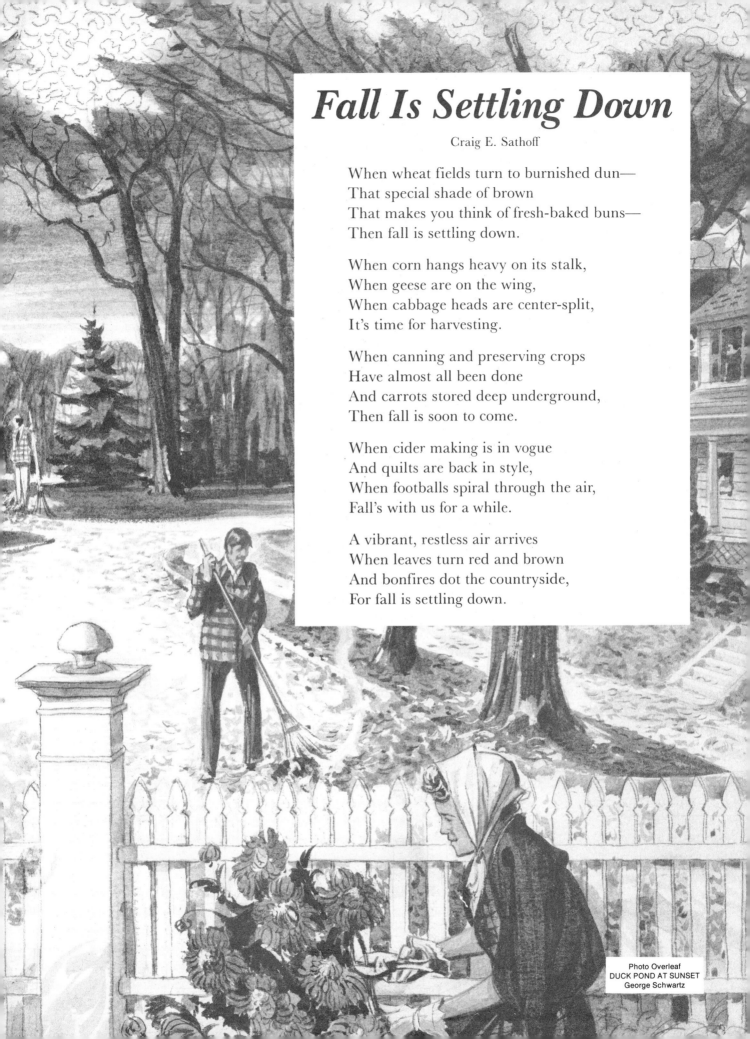

Fall Is Settling Down

Craig E. Sathoff

When wheat fields turn to burnished dun—
That special shade of brown
That makes you think of fresh-baked buns—
Then fall is settling down.

When corn hangs heavy on its stalk,
When geese are on the wing,
When cabbage heads are center-split,
It's time for harvesting.

When canning and preserving crops
Have almost all been done
And carrots stored deep underground,
Then fall is soon to come.

When cider making is in vogue
And quilts are back in style,
When footballs spiral through the air,
Fall's with us for a while.

A vibrant, restless air arrives
When leaves turn red and brown
And bonfires dot the countryside,
For fall is settling down.

Photo Overleaf
DUCK POND AT SUNSET
George Schwartz

A Slice of Life

Edgar A. Guest

When we are young, we look forward to going away. The distant city is alluring. Places far off have the charm of unfamiliarity. A trip is an adventure and the strange sights are dazzling to our eyes. The hometown and the home neighborhood seem to be commonplace in that familiarity which breeds contempt. We look upon the buildings, the parks, and even the people, without surprise or admiration.

As we grow older, especially if we have traveled much, we reverse this process of thought. We have discovered that happiness lies nearby and not far off. That what once dazzled us has lost its power to charm, and we discover that in those old familiar surroundings are all the joys that make for peace of mind. The people in the different places we have discovered are really no better and no worse than the people at home. In fact, they are very much like them with this difference: We know the home folks better. We have been on closer terms with them. We know their sorrows, we know their hopes and their aims, their virtues and their weaknesses, and by that intimate knowledge we are more comfortable in their presence. So at last I think we always come to see that the hometown, whether it be a great city or a humble one, takes its place in the mind and the imagination as the best spot on earth.

It doesn't matter much be its buildings great
   or small,
The hometown, the hometown is the best
   town, after all.
The cities of the millions have the sun and
   stars above,
But they lack the friendly faces of the few
   you've learned to love,
And with all their pomp of riches and with
   all their teeming throngs,
The heart of man is rooted in the town
   where he belongs.

There are places good to visit, there are
   cities fair to see,
There are haunts of charm and beauty
   where at times it's good to be,
But the humblest little hamlet sings a
   melody to some,

And no matter where they travel it is calling
   them to come;
Though cities rise to greatness and are gay
   with gaudy dress,
There is something in the hometown which
   no other towns possess.

The hometown has a treasure which the
   distance cannot gain,
It is there the hearts are kindest, there the
   gentlest friends remain;
It is there a mystic something seems to
   permeate the air
To set the weary wanderer to wishing he
   were there;
And be it great or humble, it still holds
   mankind in thrall,
For the hometown, the hometown, is the
   best town after all.

Pumpkin Time

Julia K. Sincak

Gathering pumpkins on the farm—
A thrilling time of year!
When we were young it meant to us
That Halloween was near.

Aunt Mary let us choose our own
From pumpkins large and small;
We clambered over golden heaps
For the smoothest one of all.

On some we'd etch a grin and sculpt
A classic friendly face;
On others, weirdest grimaces
And lone tooth left in space.

Now the smallest pumpkin face
Carved out to scare or cheer
Brings back those happy memories
Of pumpkin time each year.

Photo Opposite
PREPARATION TIME
S. Feld
H. Armstrong Roberts

On Halloween

Elisabeth Weaver Winstead

Green goblins come on Halloween,
Gray bats and black cats, too.
Hoot owls with flaming red hoot eyes
That look you through and through.

Spooks and trolls creep out of holes
And dance around their queen.
Jack-o-lantern laughs out loud
On the night of Halloween.

Mysterious figures rush about,
Then disappear from view.
Suddenly they dash right out
To shout a loud, "Guess who!"

Trick-or-treaters on the street
For this night have the freedom
To whoop and holler gathering treats,
Then drag them home and eat 'em.

A Pirate Tonight

Florence Crouse

Tonight I am a pirate
With a dagger in my teeth,
A golden earring in my ear,
A bloody scar beneath.

I swagger down the gangplank,
The scourge of every land,
Sailing o'er the seven seas
While Daddy holds my hand.

Marauding up and down the street,
Besieging every door,
Till terror-stricken villagers
Enrich my treasure store.

Then, when my ship is laden
With mounds of gold and red,
I'll sail back home to Mommy,
And she'll tuck me safe in bed.

1

2

The writings of the wise are the only riches our posterity cannot squander.

Landor

3

4

8

October is the opal month of the year. It is the month of glory, of ripeness. It is the picture month.

Beecher

9

10

A book is the only immortality.

Rufus Choate

11

15

16

Wild is the music of autumnal winds amongst the faded woods.

Wordsworth

17

18

22

Constancy is the complement of all other human virtues.

Mazzini

23

24

Think, oh, grateful, think!
How good the God of Harvest is to you;
Who pours abundance o'er your flowing fields.

Thomson

25

29

30

5

Every child walks into existence through the golden gate of love.

Beecher

6

7

Our blessings are the least heeded, because the most common events of life.

Hosea Ballou

12

13

Behold congenial Autumn comes, The Sabbath of the year!

Logan

14

19

20

21

There is one art of which man should be master—the art of reflection.

Coleridge

26

An acre of performance is worth the whole world of promise.

James Howell

27

28

Jack-O'-Lantern

Ruth Van Gorder

His face, too broad for beauty, shows
Complexion far too florid;
His eyes are vacant, and his nose
Triangular and horrid.

The spaces left between his teeth
Would shock an orthodontist;
His lid has not a hair beneath . . .
He'll win no beauty contest!

Yet when a candle set inside
Is lit, he looks quite mellow,
And very quickly we agree
That he's a charming fellow.

So other less-than-perfect creatures
(Like us) may cast a glow
And make folks quite forget our features
If we but let our light show.

Photo Opposite
JACK-O'-LANTERN WONDER
Bob Taylor

To Autumn

P. F. Freeman

Autumn with beauty our world has
   blessed,
Abundant with fruits the harvest
   brings—
Flowers of summer have gone to
   rest
Until the birth of another spring.
A roving frost has talents shown,
Changing the leaves to colors bright;
To other climates, birds have flown,
Short is the day—longer the night.

Fruits of the orchard are stored
   away,
The vegetables are in their prime,
Mows are filled with sweet-scented
   hay
At the close of harvesttime.
When beauty's blush is everywhere
As leaves to earth in silence fall,
'Tis then our world becomes aware
That autumn's the prettiest season
   of all.

Give Praise

Beverly J. Anderson

Give praise to God for autumn,
　For gold-splashed maple trees,
For gorgeous crimson sunsets,
　For woodland tapestries,
For dappled paths a-winding
　Around a peaceful hill
Where redbirds in the distance
　Glad songs of rapture spill.

Give praise to God for autumn,
　For yellow, ripened days,
For bounty of the harvest—
　Oh, let us sing God's praise!
For all of autumn's blessings
　Are gifts from God above
Who fashioned golden autumn
　And blest it with His love.

Photo Overleaf
NORTH CASCADE RANGE
Washington
Ray Atkeson

The Sumac Leaves

Jones Very

Some autumn leaves a painter took,
And with his colors caught their hues;
So true to nature did they look
That none to praise them could refuse.

The yellow mingling with the red
Shone beauteous in their bright decay,
And round a golden radiance shed,
Like that which hangs o'er parting day.

Their sister leaves, that, fair as these,
Thus far had shared a common lot,
All soiled and scattered by the breeze,
Are now by everyone forgot.

Soon, trodden under foot of men,
Their very forms will cease to be,
Nor they remembered be again
Till autumn decks once more the tree.

But these shall still their beauty boast,
To praise the painter's wondrous art,
When autumn glories all are lost
And with the fading year depart;

And through the wintry months so pale
The sumac's brilliant hues recall;
Where, waving over hill and vale,
They gave its splendor to our fall.

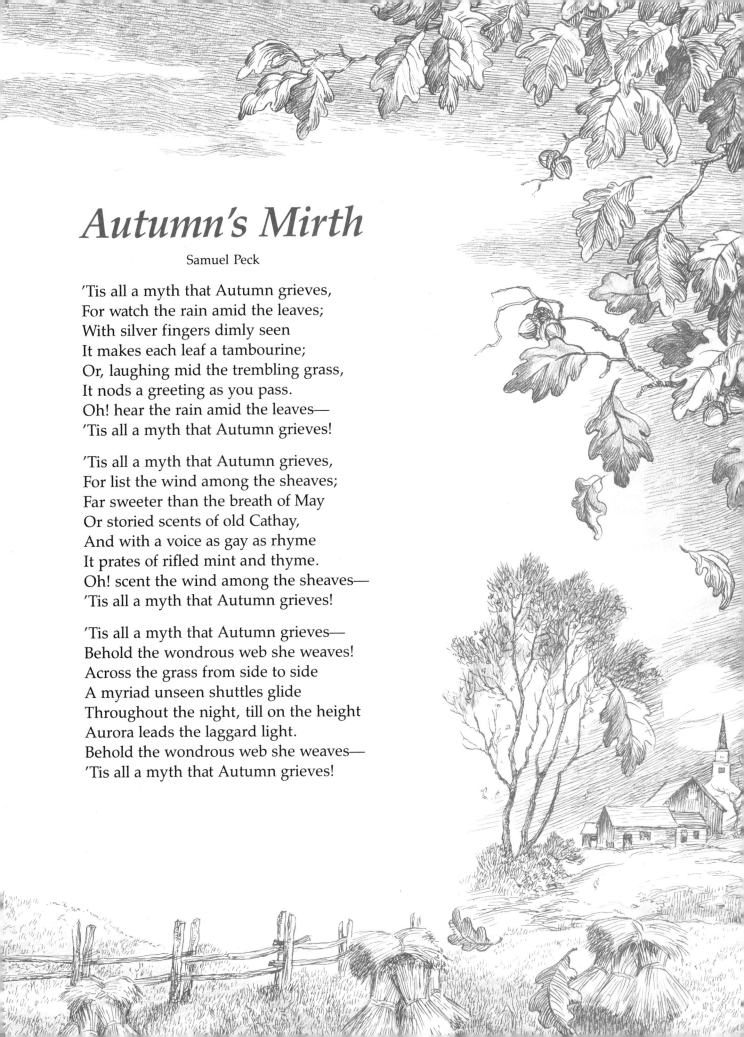

Autumn's Mirth

Samuel Peck

'Tis all a myth that Autumn grieves,
For watch the rain amid the leaves;
With silver fingers dimly seen
It makes each leaf a tambourine;
Or, laughing mid the trembling grass,
It nods a greeting as you pass.
Oh! hear the rain amid the leaves—
'Tis all a myth that Autumn grieves!

'Tis all a myth that Autumn grieves,
For list the wind among the sheaves;
Far sweeter than the breath of May
Or storied scents of old Cathay,
And with a voice as gay as rhyme
It prates of rifled mint and thyme.
Oh! scent the wind among the sheaves—
'Tis all a myth that Autumn grieves!

'Tis all a myth that Autumn grieves—
Behold the wondrous web she weaves!
Across the grass from side to side
A myriad unseen shuttles glide
Throughout the night, till on the height
Aurora leads the laggard light.
Behold the wondrous web she weaves—
'Tis all a myth that Autumn grieves!

Oh, What a Season!

Breathe deeply ... get relaxed and get ready ... *Thanksgiving Ideals* is on its way! Full of bounty to transport you into a world you will love. A world of Nature in her most brilliant finery ... a world of inspiration and hearth fires, family gatherings and the best food of the year ... a world of first snowfalls, mountain heights, and blue, blue waters.

At Ideals, we have you in mind as we put together each issue: Your thoughts. Your interests. Your enthusiasm. And we always like to hear from readers, like Ms. Marie O'Brien of Page, Nebraska, who writes:

> *If ever a magazine could be described as delicious,* Ideals *leads them all. Delicious doesn't always have to pertain to food, does it?*

Not at all, Ms. O'Brien! What a charming thought! And Mr. Robert Krug of Tavistock, Ontario, writes:

> *Subscription payment to* Ideals *is money not "well spent," but rather money "well invested," since the seasonal exquisitely beautiful issues are unfailingly an inspiration to read, and each publication provides a ray of sunshine on the day it is received.*

Thank you, Mr. Krug. With letters like this, our dedication to the highest editorial standards becomes a real commitment to you and all our valuable readers.

Come with us into a warm and wonderful world with *Thanksgiving Ideals*. It's all for you. And as we enter into a season when thanksgiving impels us to give to others, why not share your copy of *Ideals* with a friend?

ACKNOWLEDGMENTS

AS IMPERCEPTIBLY AS GRIEF by Emily Dickinson, reprinted by permission of the publishers and the Trustees of Amherst College from *THE POEMS OF EMILY DICKINSON*, edited by Thomas H. Johnson, Cambridge, Mass.: The Belknap Press of Harvard University Press, Copyright 1951 © 1955, 1979, 1983 by The President and Fellows of Harvard College; OLD APPLE HOUSE IN AUTUMN and WILD LIFE from *APPLES OF GOLD* by Grace Noll Crowell. Copyright 1950 by Harper & Row, Publishers, Inc. Reprinted by permission of Harper & Row, Publishers, Inc.; BIRCHES by Robert Frost, Copyright 1916 by Holt, Rinehart and Winston, Inc. and renewed 1944 by Robert Frost. Reprinted from *THE POETRY OF ROBERT FROST* edited by Edward Connery Lathem, by permission of Henry Holt and Company, Inc. THE HOMETOWN from *EDGAR A. GUEST BROADCASTING*, copyright 1935, The Reilly & Lee Co. Used by permission. Our sincere thanks to the following whose addresses we were unable to locate: Grace Autry for SCAMPERING LEAVES: the estate of Brian F. King for SUNSET; Julia K. Sincak for PUMPKIN TIME; Frances Cooper Thompson for REFLECTIONS.